Mommy
Why does that car
Wear a Badge?

"A story to teach children that police officers are the good guys and not the bad guys."

Mommy
Why does that car
Wear a Badge?

by D.C. Cole

ASA Publishing Corporation

ASA Publishing Corporation
An accredited hybrid book publisher with the Better Business Bureau
23 E. Front St. Suite 103, Monroe, Michigan 48161, United States of America
www.asapublishingcorporation.com

All Rights Reserved. No part of this publication may be reproduced, stored in a retrieval system or transmitted in any form or by any means electronic, mechanical, photocopying, recording or otherwise, without the prior written permission of the publisher. Author/writer rights to "Freedom of Speech" protected by and with the "1st Amendment" of the Constitution of the United States of America. This is a work of fiction with non-fiction learning ethics. Any resemblance to actual events, locales, person living or deceased is entirely coincidental. Names, places, and characters are within the work of fiction and its entirety is from the imagination of its author.

With this copyrights page, the reader is notified that this book is a children economic/educational teaching book, and the publisher does not assume responsibility, and expressly disclaims any obligation to obtain, instruct, change, and/or include any other information other than that provided by the author.

Any and all vending sales and distribution not permitted without full book cover and this title page.

Copyrights©2017 D.C. Cole, All Rights Reserved
Book: The Business Adventures of Penne' Anne' and Billy
Date Published: 12.29.2017 /Edition 1 *Trade Paperback*
Book ID: ASAPCID2380742
ISBN: 978-1-946746-24-5
Library of Congress Cataloging-in-Publication Data

This book was published in the United States of America.
State of Michigan

Mommy Why does that car Wear a Badge?

by D.C. Cole

"Mommy, why does that car have a badge on its door?"

"Well, dear that is a police car, with a police officer inside otherwise known as a "Cop"."

"He looks scary! Is he mean?"

"No Darling, he is not mean; he is the good guy."

Mommy Why does that car Wear a Badge? | 5

ASA Publishing Corporation

"But he carries a gun!"

"Yes, he does dear, he carries that for protection. He can use it to protect you from harm."

"He also has bars on his windows."

"Yes, he has bars on his windows because it protects himself from whoever is in the back seat. If he has a bad guy in the back seat those bars will keep the bad guy in the back seat. Those bars will also keep the bad guys from hurting him or causing an accident with other cars."

"But Mommy kids at my school get scared when they see a police officer. They say they are bad!"

Mommy Why does that car Wear a Badge? | **11**

ASA Publishing Corporation

"That is not true, cops are here to protect you. They only take you to jail if you break the law, and even then, they only do it if they have to. They prefer to help people, not put them in time out."

"What do you mean, Mommy?"

"Well dear, if you are ever scared or lost or feel like you are in danger and you don't see an adult you trust, you can always call them. They will come and keep you safe and bring you home. They keep the bad guys away from you."

"How do you know Mommy?"

"Well Dear, I know because they take an oath to serve and protect their community. They give up time with their families by working everyday - 24 hours a day in various shifts to make sure we are safe from harms way."

"Really?"

"Yes Darling, no matter what anyone says, you have to remember Cops are the good guys, if you ever need them, just find the closest one or call 911 and they will come to you. They will always protect you."

Mommy Why does that car Wear a Badge? | **19**

ASA Publishing Corporation

"Mom you're the best, thank you so much for telling me about Police officers. They really are our friends."

The End

www.ingramcontent.com/pod-product-compliance
Lightning Source LLC
LaVergne TN
LVHW072128070426
835512LV00002B/40